POETRY! POETRY! POETRY!

Peter Davis

POETRY!
POETRY!
POETRY!

BLOOF  BOOKS

Published by Bloof Books
www.bloofbooks.com
NEW JERSEY

Bloof Books are distributed to the trade via Ingram and other wholesalers in the US, Bertrams or Gardners in the UK, or directly from the press. Individuals may purchase them from our website, from online retailers such as Powells.com and Amazon.com, or request them from their favorite bookstores. (Please support your local independent bookseller whenever possible.)

ISBN: 978-0-9826587-0-3

CONTENTS

for Jenny

For Christ's sake, our young lad thinks, am I going to have to spend my days behind these glass walls instead of going for walks in flowery meadows? Am I going to catch myself hoping the night before each promotion exercise? Am I going to calculate, connive, champ my bit, me, who used to dream of poetry, of night trains, of warm sandy beaches?

—Georges Perec, *Things: A Story of the Sixties*

Money is a kind of poetry.

—Wallace Stevens, "Adagia"

POEM ADDRESSING THE SPECULATION AS TO WHO YOU ARE AND IMAGINING MY DEATH REAFFIRMING MY LIFE

So you like reading I imagine. And you're interested in poetry. You are probably a college undergraduate or an MFA candidate or someone interested in poems about birds or you like rhyming and whatnot. You might be a college professor. Maybe you find yourself here the same way I find myself here. Maybe you are me. If you are me, I hope you are okay with this poem today. I hope you are okay. You are likely a friend or acquaintance of mine. You may have known me in elementary school, high school, college, or grad school. You might be one of my family members. You might be my student or colleague. You might know me in some other professional/poet/artist capacity. The odds that you know me are pretty good, I think. On the other hand, by the time you read this, this poem could be slightly or barely famous. I could be eighty years old or dead and you could be a member of a government that uses this poem as a type of manual. Or you could have found these words in 2074 on a sheet of paper that is wrapped around your birthday gift. Perhaps you are thinking that the wrapping paper is better than the gift. Perhaps you haven't yet unwrapped the gift.

POEM ADDRESSING MY INTENTIONS IN THIS POEM
AND HOW I FEEL LIKE I'M DOING

It is important to me when considering this poem to do something that's easy, something that doesn't take much time or energy. I say that because this isn't the only poem I need to write. I need to write others too, to increase the possibility of publishing something. On the other hand, it's also important to me that it contains a great truth, something that will make you slow down and really think. I want you to be very impressed with this poem and the thoughts it inspires within you. I would like it to be something I'm proud of, both now, and in the future. I feel pretty good about it so far, but it's been a little harder to write than I'd hoped.

POEM ADDRESSING THE READER
AND EXPRESSING A BEAUTIFUL HOPE

I am very appreciative that you've taken the time to read this poem. I hope you like it. Let me know what I can do to improve it. I know that we all have different tastes and different ideas about what comprises good writing. Hopefully, we can agree in this instance. If you have very strong feelings about it, one way or another, you should write a review of the book in which this poem appears. If this poem is being published in a journal and you are unaware that it is also in a book, you should look it up. It is possible it is not yet in a book. You could even try reaching me, or something. You could google me. A review would really be nice. Something formal so that I feel it's legitimate. I'm actually only half interested in this poem so far, but I'm also feeling a small mania about it. I have reason to believe that I'm very, very good and that you're leaning closer and closer and closer and that at any particular instant you may kiss me on the cheek.

POEM ADDRESSING SOME OF THE OBSTACLES THIS POEM WILL FACE AS IT TRIES TO ENTERTAIN, IMPRESS, AND SUCCEED IN THE WORLD OF POETRY

Some people have ideas about outstanding poetry that don't include this sort of thing, these sorts of words, ordered up like this. Some people don't want the second sentence to mention the second sentence! There is additionally a great deal of excellent competition that this poem has to compete against for the attention of the poem reading public. My goodness, I'm amazed you're even here! I'm flabbergasted. Your reading of these words is very beautiful and, somehow, very sad, because we both know it must end. Unfortunately, that latent sadness may be an obstacle to this poem's success, too.

POEM ADDRESSING THE SELFISH NATURE OF MY THOUGHT PROCESS

What you are looking for in this poem baffles me. I am interested because I am interested in myself. I would like to see you thinking deeply about me and what I have to say. I feel that by understanding your thoughts about me, I might be able to better understand myself, which is what I'm most interested in. It would be very good if you were to review the book this poem appears in for a reputable journal. That would be good for me both professionally, and personally. Personally, I would be flattered to be taken seriously by someone who takes things seriously. Professionally, I could put your review on my vita. The more I can add to my vita the better chance I have of getting a tenure-line teaching position. I would like to be tenure-line. I would like the money and the prestige. I would also like the freedom and my summers off. If you want to review the book that this poem is in, I'm sure you could contact the publisher and they would send you a review copy. This poem might not be in a book yet. Thanks for reading the journal that this is in. It's cool of you to be so interested in poetry. I am also available for interviews and other solicitations.

POEM ADDRESSING THE OCCASION FOR WRITING

Now

POEM ADDRESSING A VERY ENTERTAINING THOUGHT

I am grateful to you for reading the first sentence of this poem. As much as I am selfish for writing it, you are generous for reading it. We can console ourselves that, if nobody else ever sees this, you and I made it at least to the end of sentence three. That must count for something. Or if this poem is now very popular and you are coming to it as reader number 50,000 or 500,000,000 you can know that you are discovering what many others have already discovered and relishing it—and you are only on sentence five! This must be very exciting for you!

POEM ADDRESSING THE READERS OF THIS POEM

You should be grateful that you're able to read this. Being able to read might not seem like much, but illiteracy is an enormous problem worldwide. I hope you live in a time when this isn't true. I hope that as a totally literate human being that you don't even know what "illiteracy" is because it simply doesn't exist in your world. That is unlikely. It is more likely that you're alive now and that you should be grateful for your ability to read. Look what it can bring you! Awesome poems like this!

POEM ADDRESSING PEOPLE WITH CERTAIN EXPECTATIONS ABOUT POETRY THAT ARE NOT FULFILLED IN THIS POEM

Change

POEM ADDRESSING POTENTIAL PUBLISHERS
OF THIS POEM, THANKS!

Perhaps you are considering this poem as part of a larger manuscript, or possibly you are considering it as a single poem or in a small group of poems for possible publication in some type of poetry-related journal. I hope you like this poem enough to publish it, obviously. That's why I've sent it to you. I'm trying to imagine how I might make it better, but I don't know what to do. Hopefully, you are thinking something like "This shit kicks serious ass!" or "This sentence is especially good. This quoting of my thoughts is terrific. Really, really good." I think it's pretty good or I wouldn't be sending it to you. Thanks for your time. Looking forward to hearing from you.

POEM ADDRESSING FURTHER SPECULATION ON THE READER AND COMMENTING ON SOME SPECIFICALLY

If you are my friend you probably say to one of our mutual friends, "What the fuck is he doing in this poem?" I don't know what you think. A lot of you may say something, but most probably won't say anything. I'd like to know. E-mail me. If you are a poet, you probably think something about this poem too. You probably don't like it. My parents have thoughts but I don't know what they are. I would hate to write something about that here since it's much more likely that they're reading this sentence than it is that you're reading this sentence.

POEM ADDRESSING MY CHILDREN

I wonder what you're thinking as you read this. If you are reading this, then it is the future now and you are just now registering the import of what I'm saying. We are together at this instant. I am only imagining and predicting this moment represented in this poem and it is giving me goose bumps. For you, you are discovering it. Like finding treasure. Of course, I don't actually have goose bumps. I'm just saying "goose bumps" to make a metaphorical point. Likewise, I'm not saying this is treasure.

POEM ADDRESSING ONE IMPORTANT REASON WHY
A LIFE IN ACADEMIA IS APPEALING TO ME

As a poet, I receive very little validation from the world. It feels good when a poem is published so that someone like you can pick this up and read it. On the other hand, what we're engaged in right here on this page is a relatively rare situation. Poetry has isolated me from the world more than it has connected me to it. My friends never really understood it and neither did my parents. But, a tenure-line teaching position is different. It says to my friends, parents, "Look! I am an impressive success!" It shows everyone around me that I'm not just some weirdo who writes, but that some accredited university or college has hired me, potentially for the rest of my career, because they think I am an asset to their highly intellectual and vital community and because they just think I'm so fucking great. That would feel nice.

POEM ADDRESSING PEOPLE WHOM I MIGHT BE ASKING
TO WRITE A BLURB FOR THE BACK COVER OF
THE BOOK IN WHICH THIS POEM APPEARS

I'm really happy this poem is in a book. I'm excited about the possibility that
you're considering this. On one hand, I hate asking for blurbs and so actively
seeking your approval. On the other hand, I like receiving approval more than
I dislike asking for it. It's embarrassing how much I crave your attention—how
much I want you to publicly acknowledge the brilliance that I display in
poems like this.

POEM THAT BEGS FOR REASSURANCE

I just
don't deserve

a Pushcart
Prize

or even a
nomination.

POEM ADDRESSING HOW I CONTINUE TO BEG FOR REASSURANCE

My experience with the world around me is that I either feel it's awful, or I feel that it is great. Right now I feel like this poem is awful. I feel like I am awful. I feel like an outcast in the literary world. Nobody reviews my work. As far as I can tell, nobody really talks about me. They do, but it's never enough. I'm not besieged with e-mails soliciting my poetry. I keep waiting for something to happen. I mean, this is a good poem. Other people seem to have so much going on. I read their bio notes and think, "Well, jeez, how do they all do it?" I say to my wife, "Honey, I always feel a few steps behind. How can I make up for all that with just a poem?" Some of these people maintain blogs with numerous links and a lot of daily hits. Others don't even have blogs! All around me poets are winning prizes and being included in anthologies like *The Best American Poetry*–some at very young ages! Some of these people, if they don't already have tenure-line teaching positions, are very strong candidates for tenure-line teaching positions!

POEM ADDRESSING HOW THE WORD *PRESTIGE* SHOULD BE DEFINED BROADLY, MEANING I'M NOT NECESSARILY JUST SEEKING TRADITIONAL FORMS OF POWER, BUT OTHER FORMS OF POWER AS WELL

It's important to me that this poem is not just shtick, but the real thing. I'm sure some people might have lots to criticize in this poem, but all that really matters to me is that there are critics. I need people to read this. The more people who read this poem, and then think and write about it, the more likely it is that I will be happy and rich and have an enjoyable job/life. It doesn't really matter what is said. I just need people to talk about me, to want poems from me, to help me out because they love my work (or because they want to make fun of it, etc.). All of this validates me as a human, plumps my ego (which is in constant need of plumping), and is excellent for my vita. Also, it is good for my ego, which constantly needs attention. I mention my ego twice (three times if you include this) because it's very important to me. Ultimately, I hope some of the attention directed at me will result in more prestige and perhaps a better job.

POEM ADDRESSING THE DEEP PAIN OF FAILURE
AND THE IMPORTANCE OF THE POEM

One thing that is horrible is that I haven't won any prestigious awards. I am hoping that this poem, or the book this poem is in, will win something fabulous, like a National Book Award or at least garner a Pushcart Prize, or be included in *The Best American Poetry*. What I'm doing in these five short sentences is pretty spectacular. I'm not bragging I'm just trying to communicate a certain idea. Also, the attention directed at the poem will feel like attention directed at my ego and so in that way this poem is responsible for my self-esteem.

POEM ADDRESSING MY AMBIVALENCE ABOUT THIS POEM

I do feel like I have important, beautiful things to say about the world, I just can't think of them at this particular instant. I don't see why you should read this poem and expect to find that sort of thing. Why look for anything in this poem? This seems like a silly place to find something.

POEM ADDRESSING POTENTIAL REVIEWERS OF MY WORK

I would be really honored if you wrote one but I don't expect it. I understand that we all have obligations and are very busy. I'm very busy writing poems like this. It's not easy.

POEM ADDRESSING SOME OF THE IDEAS THAT I THINK SHOULD BE CONSIDERED WHEN READING AND EVALUATING THIS POEM

I would like to make you more aware of yourself as a human, and thus, ultimately a better person.

I would like you to think that I'm really smart, really impressive as a person, very worthy of attention.

I would like you to be impressed with my understanding of the world.

I would like you to think that I am creative, unique, and underappreciated.

I would like to read more about myself in the popular media.

POEM ADDRESSING A FUNDAMENTAL PROBLEM OF THE ARTIST

self

is

hness

POEM ADDRESSING THE POSSIBILITY THAT I AM VOCALIZING THESE WORDS IN FRONT OF AN AUDIENCE

I hope you'll consider the very strong possibility that I have traveled to meet you here and thus you should probably buy the book this poem is in, or whatever else I might have for sale, just as a gesture of your support of the arts, in general, and, specifically, the art of poetry and the poets, like myself, who try to pull it off. I probably need the money and I have probably made a great deal of effort to write this poem and then show up here and read it to you. It's possible I haven't traveled to read this poem to you. In that case, you should buy a book from me because you probably know me and, thus, should feel obligated for weird reasons, or for reasons that aren't weird. If we're not in a poetry reading right now, and you're just reading this on your own, I hope you'll forgive all of this space devoted to the poetry reading situation. While I would enjoy vocalizing this, for the people listening, I still need to be writing this, for the people reading.

POEM ADDRESSING ENVIRONMENTAL FACTORS, SELF-HATRED, AND THE IMPORTANCE OF YOUR EXISTENCE

If you're not enjoying this poem but you're still reading it, I think you should consider a couple of things. For one, you may not be enjoying this poem for external/environmental reasons. For instance, you may be in an airport and outside they are doing construction work and there is a persistent banging that you consciously think isn't very bothersome, but, unconsciously, your body and mind may be absorbing some of the irritation created in the universe by the rather large construction equipment. Or you could have your screaming child or children clinging on your leg, wanting juice, or to eat your cigarettes, or something. It's possible you may need a cigarette, though it's more possible that if you smoke you should quit, because, ultimately, that will make you feel better and then you will be more likely to enjoy this poem. You would even feel indebted to this poem for your health! Maybe you are feeling bitter about a recent divorce or are troubled by something in a personal relationship. You may have other health or interpersonal problems. What I'm trying to say is that you might not like this poem for reasons that have nothing to do with what is written here.

POEM ADDRESSING HOW I KNEEL AT YOUR FEET, WORSHIPPING YOU BECAUSE YOU DESERVE WORSHIP

Whether you are happy with this poem or not, I appreciate you staying here with me. The thought of you is creating a kind of warmth in this basement that I'm sitting in now. Thank you for being here with me. Holding me, as it were, within the infinite hope of your plausibility. I will be beholding your beauty and your potential glory forever, which illuminates this tiny insect-like cave.

POEM ADDRESSING ASSUMPTIONS AND VARIOUS POSSIBILITIES

Since you're reading this poem, I'm assuming you're enjoying yourself. Or you feel obligated to read it. Perhaps, as a friend or student or something, you feel you must really see what this is about. You want to be fair to me as a person and so you keep plowing through it, even through this clause, intent on living up to your end of the friend-or-student-of-the-poet bargain. It would be cool for me if this poem were assigned to you in one of your college-level English classes—if so, congratulations on taking your studies so seriously. Sometimes it is only through education that we can discover stuff as cool as this poem. I hope you feel good about yourself for learning. Also, I hope you'll project some of those good feelings onto me. It's possible you might be reading this poem because you've been prodded to by your government, mom, or doctor. But I hope you're reading this mainly because you like it so much. Because you're, like, "Dude, this poem is fucking terrific!"

POEM ADDRESSING THE POSSIBILITY THAT YOU'RE
READING THIS POEM IN A LITERARY JOURNAL

Good for you. I read some journals too, but the odds of actually finding this poem can't be good. Thanks for making the effort. I hope you feel like it was worth it.

POEM ADDRESSING WAYS THAT I AM ANXIOUS AND NEEDY

It is possible you don't enjoy this poem because you have legitimate problems with the ideas and issues inherent in this poem. It is more likely that you don't enjoy this poem based on an aesthetic difference of opinion. That sort of thing happens. I hope you won't think less of me because of this.

POEM ADDRESSING WHAT I WANT TO ACCOMPLISH AND WAYS THAT YOU CAN USE THIS POEM TO ENRICH YOUR COMMUNITY

I hope you will understand that I'm only trying to write a good poem. I'm not trying to show off or do anything other than entertain you in such a way that leaves you feeling enlightened and impressed. Depending on how you feel about all of this, you may want to consider writing a reflective essay that will give you the opportunity to think more deeply about this poem. You might at least consider talking about this poem with a number of your friends, or on your blog. If you are a teacher you may want to assign it to your students and mention it to your friends in the department. Even if it seems strange, you could suggest forming a reading club devoted to this poem and the complex and simple issues it illuminates.

POEM ADDRESSING DOUBTS THAT ARE ILLUMINATED, BEFORE SHIFTING THE ATTENTION TO YOU, BEFORE SHIFTING IT BACK TO ME AGAIN

I want to explain more about what I'm thinking, but I'm afraid it will make me seem stupid. I do worry about how I appear in this poem. It is not cool for a poet to appear to be anxious for praise and attention in a poem. It is not cool for anyone to appear to be anxious for praise and attention. I'm just saying something that is true. I hope you will not hold that against me, or this poem. I would suggest that if you do not feel that you, or those you admire, are anxious for praise and attention then you are not looking at yourself and the world realistically. Of course, I'm not interested in saying insightful, realistic things, which I wouldn't say except for the fact that I'm interested in saying insightful, realistic things.

POEM ADDRESSING SIDES OF MYSELF I REALLY
DON'T LIKE TO THINK ABOUT

I'm probably envious of you, whoever you are. You probably have something I want. You might live in a beautiful house, or be published by a prestigious press, or might have a sweet teaching position somewhere super cool. I don't know. Sometimes I think I am cooler than everyone. Sometimes I think you're so lame. I look at myself as special. Sometimes I can't believe how little I'm appreciated by you. How could you not notice how cool this poem is? How couldn't you see? I don't know how to feel about you because I don't know how to feel about myself. I have this rage that I can't explain. It's sad.

POEM ADDRESSING PEOPLE WHO MIGHT HIRE ME FOR THEIR TENURE-LINE TEACHING POSITION BUT ARE UNSURE ABOUT WHAT THEY'RE READING

No worries. This doesn't change the fact that I'd be a terrific teacher for you and an asset to your community. I'm a trustworthy and dependable colleague and I've been teaching for years as an adjunct. I get excellent student evaluations!

POEM ADDRESSING SOME OF MY BORING WISHES

I am very interested in what you have to say about this poem. If you, for instance, have a problem with this sentence, I would like to know what it is. If you have a problem with this sentence, I would like to know why, and if it differs at all from the problems you might have had with the previous sentence. The best way to do this would be in the form of a review in a literary journal, in print or on the web. I google myself daily and will surely notice what you write. You could also send me an e-mail: artisnecessary@yahoo.com.

POEM ADDRESSING MY CHILDREN REGARDING MY INTENTIONS
AS AN ARTIST, ESPECIALLY IN THIS POEM

I am hoping to be writing something now that you are proud of. I hope you think that this poem is courageous and written with love. I hope you realize that I'm trying to set an example of bravery, persistence, dedication, and love with this poem. I hope all of that is coming through. It is very possible that this sentence doesn't seem brave to you at all, but I hope you'll understand how hard it is to write a brave, decent poem. I'm trying. I hope you'll try. I don't mean that you should try to write a brave, decent poem, but just that when you try anything, I hope you will think of this poem and how hard I am trying to set a good example with it.

POEM ADDRESSING BABIES

Isn't this a good poem? O yes, it is a very good, good poem! This poem is a very, very, very good poem! O, yes it is. Yes it is! O, yes it is. What do you think, honey? What are you thinking, baby? O baby sweet baby. Yes, that's a sweet baby. Are you smiling baby? Yes! O yes you're smiling, aren't you? Cutie. You're such a cutie. My goodness, aren't you a cutie? Isn't this a good poem? Yes, it's a good poem. Yes it is. Whose fat little cheeks are those? Are those your fat little cheeks? O, you're a sweetie. Sweetie pie, sweetie pie. My little cutie, fat cheeks. My little pretty pie. O yes, it is a good poem. O yes it is! It is a good, good poem!

POEM ADDRESSING BOYS, AGE 5

This poem can turn invisible and it can beat up bad guys! When people read this poem it is like a laser shooting bad guys right in the stomach! This poem knocks bad guys on their bottoms! And if you need a force field you can get one from Dr. Defense who lives in this poem and makes a number of bad-guy-fighting tools and weapons. Sometimes giant robot bad guys try to kill this poem by bopping it on the head, but this poem doesn't allow that and sends ninjas and wizards out to reverse time and destroy the robots. Dr. Defense jumps up and kicks everyone in the face and he, like, flies through a window and then, like, this poem explodes!

POEM ADDRESSING PEOPLE READING THIS UNDERWATER

This is a strange place for you to be reading a poem. And the odds that you're reading poetry underwater and you come across a poem that is about that situation! Fantastic! The universe can be incredible! Just try to take this moment in. This is really something!

POEM ADDRESSING PEOPLE WHO LIKE NARRATIVE POEMS INVOLVING EPIPHANIES AND CUTE STUFF PRESENTED IN A MILDLY SURREALISTIC WAY

Once there was this poem that began with a long title and a rather obvious beginning sentence. It was a good poem, a kind poem, a poem that always thought of others. At one moment, there was a knock on the door of the poem. When the poem answered the door it found an animal that was exceedingly common in nearly every area of the world, except in the area where the poem lived. The poem, surprised by the sight of this animal, dropped the glass it was holding, severing its toes. The animal leapt on the bleeding stumps, sucking the blood of the poem, getting fatter and fatter. When the poem ended, things were different somehow. The poem had a rainbow over it and was holding a bunny and watching a baby smile for the first time.

POEM ADDRESSING MY POETRY FRIENDS AND WHATNOT, MY CONTEMPORARIES WITH WHOM I MEET AND CONVERSE

I mostly feel inferior. Many of you are smart and good-looking and, more importantly, obviously very "cool." Some of you won something prestigious or went to some super great school or something. I like to think that I am very "cool" but I question myself sometimes when I am around you. Other times, I feel that you are pretentious or too serious or too something or too stupid. Sometimes I feel superior to you. Sometimes I don't enjoy being with you because all of us can be so self-conscious. This makes for some awkward stuff sometimes. Thank goodness we all drink so much!

POEM ADDRESSING CONTEMPORARY POETS OF WHOM I'VE BEEN JEALOUS ON MORE THAN ONE OCCASION

I'm really sorry about this and embarrassed. I'm only mentioning it because it makes for a decent poem. Of course, you might not think so. Sorry, again.

POEM ADDRESSING MY CONTEMPORARIES, MANY OF WHOM I AM COMPETING AGAINST FOR SWEET TEACHING POSITIONS

I really hope you like this. What you think of me really matters to me. I want you to just love this and write reviews of it and talk it up on your blog. That would make me feel really good. If you've got students, I hope you'll be teaching them this poem and, if this poem appears in a book, I hope you'll make them buy it for the class. I'll come there for a reading! Seriously, I love that kind of thing! But, of course, also, I understand that many of you will be underwhelmed by this poem. You might not even enjoy the way I'm talking to you in this sentence and using a word like *underwhelmed*. If that's the case, I apologize. I wish this were a poem you really enjoyed. Still, in any case, if you dislike it, I hope you dislike it enough to write a negative review of it for a reputable journal. Just be fair. I can't promise that I will write a fair review of your work, but if you're ever coming through my town let me know, and I'll try to set up a reading for you. Good luck with the job search. See you at AWP!

POEM ADDRESSING MY CONTEMPORARIES
OF WHOM I AM UNAWARE

I like making friends but I'm not very good at it. I could improve on that aspect of my life. This is an awkward gesture, but I hope you'll accept it.

POEM ADDRESSING PEOPLE WHO HAVE ACTUALLY
DECIDED TO WRITE A REVIEW OF THIS

Thanks! I'm so happy that you exist! You are crucial in establishing my reputation as a poet. Without your help, I'm nothing really. Thank you, again. I'm sure that you understand how flattering it is to read about myself in the third person, to know that people in this world are thinking about me—about what I'm thinking, about what I think. I am very concerned with what I think. My thoughts are really all I think about. I try not to think of my thoughts, to unload them from myself, but I can't. I always find them again. This poem is an example of me trying to unload my thoughts—to be free from them, for just a moment. As it turns out, I am only free from them when other people are carefully considering them, and I, in turn, am carefully considering those people. Only then can I really be me! At those moments, I'm free. At those moments, I really find myself. Those small moments I owe to you, actual reviewer!

POEM ADDRESSING MY PAST, CURRENT AND FUTURE STUDENTS WHO ARE SUFFICIENTLY INTERESTED IN OUR CLASS TO CHECK OUT MY WORK

I hope you learn something from this poem and the powerful, mystical way it concludes!

POEM ADDRESSING PEOPLE WHO READ MY FIRST BOOK
OF POEMS, SO ARE CHECKING THIS OUT

Sorry to ask even more of you, but maybe you could make some sort of pledge
to yourself that you'll tell X number of people about my work and this poem?
Something simple. You'd be surprised how easy it is to make me feel better.
Even if you only mentioned me once a day, I'd still feel very appreciative.

POEM ADDRESSING THE POSSIBILITY THAT THIS POEM
IS BEING READ AS SOME SORT OF BROADSIDE

I think it would be great! I could put it on my vita and you, reader of this poem, could treat these words as a sort of cultural referent point, referring others to them to show the serious degree to which you are engaged in contemporary American poetry. You may also be reading this poem as it hangs vertically on a wall! Fantastic! I hope you are inside the home of a famous poet and you're reading this as it hangs on his or her wall. If that's the case, please let me know. Even better, you could write an article for a reputable journal about reading this poem as it hung inside of a famous poet's house. Wow! That'd all feel great!

POEM ADDRESSING THE POSSIBILITY THAT I'M READING THIS POEM AS PART OF A PRESENTATION THAT IS DIRECTED TOWARD GRADUATE STUDENTS, MY COLLEAGUES, AND SOME OF MY STUDENTS

Oh, this makes me nervous! I want to be smart and funny and illuminating. I want people to enjoy this poem and feel like it was worth their time. I know some people won't like it and that's okay with me. In the question-and-answer portion of this presentation, I will be happy to address your concerns. I hope you'll tell me about them and why you feel so strongly about this poem. Knowing you have strong feelings will make me feel better. It's okay with me if you don't like this. You don't have to come up to me and say, "That was interesting" or something, you can just say you don't like it. I'm not even sure that I like it. However, the point is really that the best way to register your displeasure with this poem is to write a formal review of it for a well-respected journal. Many of you could advance your own career and reputation by writing a review of this and, by so doing, help me advance my career and reputation. Making a living is very important and we all know that. Anyway, I hope you like this poem. I am hoping that this poem is the greatest thing you've ever heard.

POEM ADDRESSING THE NATURE OF THE LITERAL AND THE
METAPHORICAL, MAKING THE IMPORTANCE OF YOUR ROLE CLEAR

If you don't want to be wrong, I am absolutely taking it for granted that you are right all of the time. I am grateful for your consistency and for being able to count on you in this way. It means a great deal to me as the writer of this poem to know that your opinion of this poem is completely correct. Of course, I know it is possible that you are affected by circumstances that have nothing to do with these words, but are more likely related to environmental or historical factors. But what I'm saying now, and the important point to take away from this poem, is: I trust you. When it's all over, no matter what, I trust that you understand and are always right.

POEM ADDRESSING MY DESPERATION

Please, if you are a human who contributes to the world of poetry, ask me to contribute to your journal, or request a manuscript, or invite me for a reading, or write a review of my work, or help get me hired at your university, or send me something supportive or something. I'm a castaway who needs a bottle with a message in it. Okay? Are times that hard for my ego? Yes. Float me something, people who attend AWP and are interested in contemporary American poetry! Give me a reason to believe in myself!

POEM ADDRESSING KITTENS

Here kitty kitty. Here kitty kitty kitty

POEM ADDRESSING PEOPLE WHO ARE READING THIS POEM IN SOME SORT OF HARDBOUND ANTHOLOGY

Well, this feels pretty good. I've always wanted this poem to be in this situation. It is most likely very clear to you why this poem has been included. Either for its historical significance or the way it is a useful example of the many things poems are capable of (techniques, theories, etc.). This may be included because I am friends with the editor or friends with someone who is really good friends with the editor. It is possible that this poem is being used as an example of what's bad about poetry, but that doesn't seem likely given the fact that it's so good and insightful. I hope this isn't the only poem of mine being represented in this anthology, but if it is, I hope it's enough to convince you that I'm terrific, causing you to seek out my work, my books, etc. and ultimately causing you to write a review of this, or at least get you to write me personally and tell me how much you like this poem. I hope there are many prestigious writers in this anthology. That would really make me feel good. If I were to appear numerous times in many prestigious anthologies with many prestigious writers and artists, I think that would go a long way in repairing those awful feelings about myself that I've had for, like, forever.

POEM ADDRESSING PEOPLE WHO ARE EDITING
SOME NEW ANTHOLOGY

This would be a great poem for something like that.

POEM ADDRESSING PEOPLE WHO ARE WAITING SOMEWHERE
FOR SOMETHING AND SO ARE READING THIS POEM
JUST TO KILL THE TIME

It's cool that you have a cool poem like this to read in a pinch! This should help pass the time for the next few moments and you can read this again if you still have time to when it's over. Also you can probably view whatever else is in the publication you are holding in your hands. Of course you might not be reading this poem as a piece in a bound publication. These are the ways I imagine you might be reading this: in a book, in a magazine/journal, on your computer, on a single sheet of paper (broadside maybe?). It does occur to me that you might be waiting in a public place that is a notorious public space in which waiting occurs—like a doctor's office, a bank, some kind of government building, an airport, a subway station, etc. In that case, it is possible that whoever manages this space has considered writing this poem on the wall, or printing it on a banner or something, just to entertain you. Someone cool, somewhere down the line, said to someone else who was cool, "Hey there's this great poem I know about that would be great to put in the waiting room." This seems unlikely for reasons that are very obvious. A simple logistical problem would be the length of this poem. Even though you're only this far in you can probably tell, just by glancing at the text, that this poem continues quite a while past this sentence. Of course, that problem could be solved if this poem were running on some kind of digital scroll, like stock prices across Times Square or the ticker tape at the bottom of a television news channel. So, there are ways that this could be accomplished if people really devoted some thought and time to it. Anyway, I hope this is helping you and that whatever you're waiting for is no big deal. I mean, I hope you're just cashing your paycheck or something and not waiting to hear whether you have cancer or not. And, if that's what you're doing now (or something else that's awful, like waiting for a verdict in a case, or on a wayward friend)—anyway, I wish you luck. I hope all will be well for you. I think the odds that you're reading this while waiting for something extremely awful and serious are pretty slim. Not many people read poetry when they're nervous. And, when they do, they rarely get anything out of it. Since you're this far into the poem, you must be getting something out of it. And though I'm just trying to kill some time with you, I still want this poem to be something that you can get something out of. So, concentrate. Really think about this poem. You don't want to be thinking about the clock. Think about this poem and the time will just fly by.

POEM ADDRESSING PEOPLE WHO HAVE INVITED ME
TO PARTICIPATE IN THEIR READING SERIES

That's great. I like to do that type of thing. It's a very good feeling for me to be wanted and listened to. Of course, I'd love it if you financially compensated me in some way, but really, I consider the boost to my ego compensation enough. Thanks for your efforts and for including me.

POEM ADDRESSING PEOPLE WHO WOULD LIKE ME
TO CONTRIBUTE TO THEIR REALLY COOL JOURNAL

I hope you're asking me because by the time you read this I'm a well-respected poet, a really big deal, teaching at a prestigious university, admiring the awards that hang on my wall. I might be a real dick by now. If I'm ignoring your e-mails or blowing you off in some other way, just remind me of this poem. Surely showing your knowledge of my earlier work will feed my ravenous ego enough to get me to send you something.

POEM ADDRESSING ACADEMICS WHO ARE CONSIDERING WRITING A DISSERTATION OR A BOOK ABOUT THIS POEM

I think this is the perfect poem for something like that. I'm sure you get what I'm saying. While this poem doesn't overtly delve into theory, it certainly can inform such a discussion a great deal. Also, it can shed a great deal of light on other issues that are relevant to contemporary poetry and other various germane aspects of human culture. For instance, you might want to consider this poem and its relationship to: Melville, William Carlos Williams, Emily Dickinson, peace, consciousness, ego, psychology, Freud, Gertrude Stein, happiness, success, movement, cartoons, Raymond Queneau, Joe Wenderoth, post-pre-post-modernism, aesthetics, surface, resurface, biography, smallness, George Perec, Kenneth Goldsmith, Bob Dylan, Roger Miller, orange, New York City, Randy Newman, avant sneakers, peeled stuff, United States history, other colors, world chicken, Aism, Bism, Cism, Dism, Etc.ism, jazz, other jive, Otherism, speech, talking, pathology, and pyramids. Of course this poem is relevant to many more subjects and disciplines, but these are the ones that immediately spring to mind.

POEM ADDRESSING PREDILECTIONS AND REVEALING FANTASIES ABOUT THE READER

I'm so glad the idea of sex has entered into this poem. I love sex. What I like about it is how sexy it is. Print and television advertisements have shown us that things with sex in them are way better than things without sex. Now that this poem is including sex it will be more marketable. It might come up in more Google searches. It will have an additional draw. In addition to the excellent writing and smart ideas of the poem, it will also show graphic home movies in the reader's mind. Most readers, by this point in time, are already thinking about some form of genitalia and some readers who are more adventurous and spontaneous are even masturbating, or thinking about masturbating.

POEM ADDRESSING ANY THERAPIST I MIGHT HAVE WHO IS READING THIS AS SOME SORT OF WINDOW TO FIGURING SOMETHING OUT ABOUT ME

I appreciate it that you're taking the time to read this poem. It shows you're dedicated to your profession and, specifically, me. That's good of you. Thank you. I don't know what exactly this poem will show about me that will be of use to you. I hope something. I do value your opinion or advice or I wouldn't be seeing you. It's even possible that I've given you the book this poem appears in, or just given you this poem because I thought you might get a kick out of it. Hope you are. When I imagine this I realize that I might be watching you now, having just handed this to you, and you are gazing down at these words now, while I am eyeing you or looking out the window or at the window blinds. This might make for an awkward situation. I have a talent for awkward situations. (That sounds like something you might be able to use.) But, on the other hand, I might not be watching you now. Perhaps I gave this to you earlier and you're just reading it now. Perhaps you found this independently in a journal or a book. I hope you've found something useful. I'm counting on your help.

POEM ADDRESSING MY ELEMENTARY, JUNIOR HIGH, AND HIGH SCHOOL TEACHERS

I'm very surprised that you're reading this. I can imagine a chain of events that might get these words before your eyes at this moment, but every sequence I can fathom is unlikely and far-fetched. I can't imagine who you might be now. But we find ourselves here, grown adults, one of whom was a student of the other. Now it seems we are in a different situation. You most likely know nothing about contemporary American poetry. (I'm really, really amazed that you're reading this!) I hope you feel like you're learning something. I hope you can appreciate the contribution that I'm making to contemporary American poetry. If you can identify a certain phrase or word in this poem that you feel was surely the result of your teaching, please consider yourself a contributor to contemporary American poetry, too! It's a pretty easy club to join!

POEM ADDRESSING PEOPLE WHO DON'T LIKE POETRY
BUT ARE GIVING IT A SHOT WITH THIS POEM

I mean, you've made it this far into the first sentence, so you must be having some fun. How fun is this? It's great! Hilarious! I hope you can't read this sentence because your eyes are watering from laughter. Of course, actually, I hope you can still read this because that's the important thing about poetry.

POEM ADDRESSING PEOPLE WHO ARE READING THIS
FOR THE THIRD OR FOURTH TIME

I've heard that good poems reward you again, and again, each time you read them. I basically believe that too. So, by now, I'm guessing you're pretty blown away.

POEM ADDRESSING TEENAGERS WHO ARE NEW
TO READING POETRY

Seriously, some poetry fucking rocks, like this poem! You see what I mean? I mean, you might be thinking, seriously, dude, I didn't know poetry could be this fucking cool. But it is so fucking cool. It is so fucking cool, motherfuckers! It's better than a movie cause most movies suck. And it's better than TV because TV sucks! And fuck yeah, some poems suck, but this one doesn't. It kicks ass! Fucking A!

POEM ADDRESSING PEOPLE OF VARIOUS NATIONS

I'm not sure in what way, but I feel certain this poem is relevant to you and your country. This isn't an American poem, despite the fact that I'm from the United States. In fact, I think in many ways it's very un-American. Not so much in the first two sentences, or even this one, but the third sentence really makes that clear.

POEM ADDRESSING THE POSSIBILITY THAT THE UNITED STATES GOVERNMENT HAS FORCED YOU TO READ THIS POEM

I'm sorry you're being forced to read this; on the other hand, it feels really great to be needed. I feel so vindicated.

POEM ADDRESSING DICTATORS

We're similar to the extent that I try to control everything in this poem and you try to control everything wherever you are. I'm excited that you're reading this because it's a good poem and you are in the position to promote it beyond my wildest imagination. I hope you won't be violent as you impose this on your people, but I do hope you will gently incorporate this poem into your society, letting it bring your people its subtle reassurance. I am ultimately on the side of your people and hope that they achieve freedom from you, some autonomy as a people. I want them to understand that I am with them in this poem. But I also want you, Good Leader, to give them this poem as a gift. I know you're probably not accustomed to giving gifts and taking suggestions, but, since you're already reading a contemporary American poem, which can't be something you do often, you might as well try something else that's different too.

POEM ADDRESSING CONSPIRACY THEORISTS

You're right to understand the underlying devious intentions of this poem. You are definitely on to something. You should really examine my other poems too (just google me) and notice the clues I have left behind. You might want to share what you find with others by starting a blog, informing the media, making videos, etc. I have said to my wife and others that I don't understand how few people notice the prophecy in my work. For reasons that are probably obvious to you, I don't want to directly address what I'm not openly addressing, except to say that, yes, I am addressing what you think I am. I know; it blows my mind too!

POEM ADDRESSING THE POSSIBILITY THAT I'M READING THIS AS PART OF THE INAUGURATION CEREMONY FOR THE PRESIDENT OF THE UNITED STATES

Wow, this is quite an honor! I'm delighted to be here and very, very grateful to be included in this historic event. I'm sure many of you listening to this (or reading this) know very little about poetry and are surprised by what you're hearing (or reading) and wondering, essentially, "Why are we listening to these words right now? Why is this a poem and what are we, as a nation, supposed to take away from this?" Well, for one thing I want to point out what a good thing this situation is for me. I get very little recognition as poet and now I will go down in (some) history books and I will probably be able to secure any academic job I might need based on the sheer coolness of this gig! And for this, I thank (and I think you should too) our new president!

POEM ADDRESSING ECONOMISTS

The problem with this poem, from your perspective, must be its lack of financial value. I guess my problem with you, from my perspective, is how you insist on putting a financial value on everything. But you're right, I guess. In fact, despite the odds, I hope this poem is worth a great deal financially. And, if that's not possible, I want it to pay off emotionally. Perhaps you can come up with some financial incentives or deterrents that will move this poem into the commercial marketplace. Everyone, including you and me, would have a lot more respect for this poem if you could.

POEM ADDRESSING CHRISTIANS AND
THE CONCEPT OF FORGIVENESS

You might think I need Jesus, but you and I most likely know that this poem will do just fine in place of Jesus. If you don't like blasphemy, I'm sorry; I never meant to hurt you!

POEM ADDRESSING THE POSSIBILITY THAT THIS POEM IS BEING READ IN CONNECTION WITH A FESTIVAL FOR GREGORY CORSO

This is terrific! I'm so excited to be a part of this event. Any event celebrating the idea of poetry is terrific, and, if the event includes me, I feel that it is especially noteworthy. Also, it's great to celebrate Gregory Corso. There have been enough festivals devoted to Allen Ginsberg and Jack Kerouac, but, while I've never been invited to participate in festivals for them, I've never been invited to a festival for Corso even more frequently. Until now! So the universe is really coming together for Corso and me. I'd never thought of it like that before, but now I'm really starting to see the way that he and I were always sort of pointed toward this moment, coming together now, in the unbreakable bond that is this poem and this reading. How cool for Corso to be honored by us younger, still-alive, poets. This is just the sort of thing he needs to further establish his reputation in the world of poetry. What's great too is how when I have to fill out my annual report for the university at which I work, I can put my attendance at this festival on my vita. This will surely impress the committee that evaluates my yearly performance. Maybe I'll even get a raise! I just can't see a downside to this festival, except, maybe, the way this poem ends, all suddenly melancholy and strangely sentimental.

POEM ADDRESSING PEOPLE WHO WILL NEVER READ THIS

It's funny that I'd write this for you, I think. I mean, I don't understand why I do anything. This poem is a really good example of that.

POEM ADDRESSING WHY I CHOOSE TO WRITE POEMS
WHEN I KNOW IT IS A HIGHLY UNLIKELY WAY
TO RECEIVE THE APPROVAL I CRAVE

My need for approval is such that even normal approval is not good enough. I only feel good about approval if I have earned it in the hardest way I can imagine. If you, by some amazing stroke of luck, find this poem and it impresses you so much that you feel very positive about me, and if you communicate that positive feeling to me, I will feel very good for a very short period of time (especially if you are well-respected and/or semi-famous). I wait for this rare and fleeting event because I can't think of anything else worth waiting for. It's sad.

POEM ADDRESSING THE VERY NUMEROUS INSTANTS THAT CLING TOGETHER, FORMING AN ENORMOUS ROPE OF LIFE THAT IS GOOFY AND STRANGE

You are as beautiful as this poem, but shorter.

POEM ADDRESSING THE ELDERLY

If you fit the stereotype of the elderly then you're either oblivious to what you're reading or you don't understand it or you just don't like it. I hope none of those things are the case. If you've registered the import of that last sentence, then you are likely really here with me now. This is what I was hoping for. It's beautiful to transcend generations and to just be inside an artistic work, together, enjoying what only a great artistic work can provide.

POEM ADDRESSING REALTORS

You should try to sell this poem as a place where a person could metaphorically live. Show it to a number of clients, give those clients fact sheets about the poem, encourage them to get an inspection of the poem and to ask for a poem warranty. Aside from that, just try to stay out of the way of the beauty of the poem and put a good spin on its abrupt ending.

POEM ADDRESSING LAW ENFORCEMENT OFFICERS

You could try reading this poem to some of the suspects you arrest. I think it would express a sense of humanity on your part and thus may show your suspect that a sense of humanity may seem like a strange concept in this particular situation, but that it's also very important. If you're reading this to a suspect now, I would like to directly address him or her: Dude, really take in the oddness of this situation—that a cop is reading you a poem! Not only is a cop reading you a poem, but it's about you. I wrote this for the officer, but I also wrote this to you, arrestee! This is an opportunity, man. Take it!

POEM ADDRESSING REAL SICKOS

You know, I just don't know what your deal is. I can't imagine why you would read a poem. But, I guess that sort of unpredictability is part of your whacko psychology. Anyway I wish this poem could reference or portray the type of sickness that would both gratify and reform you. I don't want you to be violent or depressed or whatnot. I want you engaged in this poem and entertained (with your eviscerations, exploding bones, etc.), but I also want you to become unsick, to not be a sicko. You sickos make me sick! I just want to change this vicious cycle!

POEM ADDRESSING FANS OF CELINE DION

I look at myself in the mirror all the time, as you might, and I just think, what the fuck?

POEM ADDRESSING THE CAST MEMBERS OF *BEVERLY HILLS, 90210*

Wow, I can't imagine how this poem would find you Jennie Garth, Tori Spelling, Luke Perry, Jason Priestley, Ian Ziering, Shannen Doherty, Brian Austin Green, Gabrielle Carteris, Carol Potter, James Eckhouse, Joe E. Tata, and Tiffani-Amber Thiessen. Maybe you read poetry journals or books of contemporary poetry, but I doubt it. I imagine you've found this through the internet somehow. Perhaps this poem will be in some online literary journal and you are googling your name and going through, like, EVERY hit that comes up and so you find yourself here, in this poem, wondering what is coming next.

POEM ADDRESSING THE ILLITERATE

I am glad this is finding you, despite the obvious difficulties. I hope this might inspire you to learn to read. I hope that whoever is helping you with this poem becomes a close friend to you, in such a way that your relationship naturally leads to an educational bond. Not everything that is written is as fascinating and life-changing as this poem, but there is some pretty good stuff out there.

POEM ADDRESSING THE UNLIKELY POSSIBILITY THAT THIS POEM IS BEING USED IN SOME KIND OF MEDIATION PROCESS

I'm not sure what value this poem can have in these proceedings. Good luck to everyone. I hope you all get what you need, which, of course, requires that you also probably need to give something up. But no one needs to give up how much they enjoy this poem! Without sacrificing a thing, we can all love this equally! This is super feel-good and brings us all a little closer together!

POEM ADDRESSING BMX BIKE RIDERS AND
SKATEBOARDERS OF THE 1980s

Dudes, you are about as radical as anything I know. Your checkered Vans are totally awesome! I'm stoked by your fresh moves and fluorescent sweatshirts. Dude, it's insane! You're, like, so freaking gnarly! Seriously holmeses, it's way rad that you're reading cool poetry these days!

POEM ADDRESSING PEOPLE READING THIS WHO HAVE BEEN SITTING TOO LONG IN A CHAIR TO ENJOY THIS POEM

When this happens to me, I always get up and walk around a bit. It just works.

POEM ADDRESSING PEOPLE READING THIS WHILE LYING IN BED

Sometimes when people read in bed they end up falling asleep. This poem will be short to keep that from being a problem. Stay alert! I would hate to think of you drifting off before this poem was over and thus missing this super transformative moment right here at the end!

POEM ADDRESSING PEOPLE WHO HAVE BEEN RECENTLY INJURED OR ARE IN GREAT PHYSICAL OR PSYCHOLOGICAL PAIN

Put this poem down and take care of yourself! I know this poem is good and ultimately more important than your health, but, for now, just this instant, your well-being is more important. All I ask is that, when you're better, you tell people about this poem. You could do something simple like write a review of this for a reputable journal, or maybe do something deeper, like develop a theory or philosophy about this poem and how it helped you heal and how it might help others.

POEM ADDRESSING PEOPLE WHO ARE TIRED, HUNGRY, OR HORNY

These things can wait. This is a very good poem and you'd be very myopic to lose sight of this beauty simply because some of your baser needs are asserting themselves. I'll keep this short, but you should exercise some control, okay? Stay with me here. Allow this poem to carry you beyond yourself, transcending your mortal flesh as you wed yourself with the potentially infinite.

POEM ADDRESSING FAMOUS TELEVISION AND FILM STARS

I feel certain that working this poem into one of your projects wouldn't be that hard. It might not seem like much to you, but to me, it would be a tremendous boon to my career and, I think, to poetry, in general. Also, this wouldn't be just for me, you would get to be associated with great literature—poetry, for god's sake, and that'd be cool for you too! It'll smarten up your public image a shitload!

POEM ADDRESSING REALLY COOL, POPULAR MUSICIANS

If you want to turn this poem into a popular song, that's cool with me. I hope it's a big hit! I just want to be financially compensated in some way. Thanks for this. Poets don't make much money and this should help my family and me a lot.

POEM ADDRESSING PEOPLE WHO LOVE HEAVY METAL
BUT DON'T KNOW ANYTHING ABOUT POETRY

It's interesting that you find yourself here. Important things to remember: You can get stoned to this poem, bang your fucking head to this poem, and raise your fist in the air and rock to this poem! If this poem is too loud, you're too old! And you call yourself hardcore. Fucking pussy!

POEM ADDRESSING TREES IN AUTUMN

I bet you're getting a little chilly. Slowly emptying yourself of your leaves. Getting brittle and more shivery every instant. You're probably, like, "Burrrrrr, getting cold up in here." It's kind of like this poem, how it trickles onward, showing more and more of itself as it whittles itself further and further away. One can't ever be sure what is more valuable: what has gone away, or what remains. Yikes! This poem is sounding like a Led Zeppelin song! Sucky!

POEM ADDRESSING PEOPLE THAT WORK FOR AN ARTS ORGANIZATION AND ARE CONSIDERING INVITING ME TO BE A GUEST ARTIST AT SOME SORT OF EVENT THEY ARE ORGANIZING

One thing that's true about me is that I'm easygoing and willing to work with you. I'm not looking to make money, really, I just want to feed my own ego. Ergo, I am willing to be very accommodating as long as I'm invited and treated with a modicum of respect. Also, I'm really good at this sort of thing—talking in front of people, especially if it's about me or my work, or if I can relate the subject back to me and my work. Anyway, I dare you: Find a better bang for your buck than me. I'm sorry, that dare seems egotistical. I'm not egotistical. Or, rather, I'm not more egotistical than most other people. I won't be a problem is all I mean. I hope you'll understand that all I mean is: Take a chance on me, even though that chance is a safe bet. I'm trying to sell myself while maintaining some humility. This sort of thing is hard for me. I just want you to like me. I just want you to see how good we might be together.

POEM ADDRESSING SOME OF THE FRUSTRATION OF A POET

This poem isn't very good. This sentence doesn't say what I want it to say. This poem doesn't sound right. I don't feel right about this. I feel terrible about all of this. I can't believe I do this. It's stupid I do this. It doesn't make sense. I hate myself. I can't stand what happens in my brain. It's all driving me crazy! I'm tired of it. The worst thing about this poem is all of these words. I can't stand these words. These words are driving me crazy!

POEM ADDRESSING HOW WE READ THIS

Already my conscious mind is beginning to digest this poem and is beginning to spit out little opinions. Yours probably is too. In nearly every case, this is probably a bad thing. Let's try to quit that. Just relax and enjoy how beautiful this last part is.

POEM THAT BELLIGERENTLY ADDRESSES PEOPLE WHO BELIEVE I'M SELF-OBSESSED OR SOMETHING LIKE THAT

Well, you have an enormous ego too. That's why you're reading this, you narcissist! Get over yourself! Sure, you're smart because you get what this poem is about and how cool it is, or you get how crappy this poem is, and you know why, but you're still just another reader. So, don't look at me. You're the one obsessed with yourself!

POEM ADDRESSING HOPE AND PRACTICALITY, WHICH MIGHT BE SAID TO BE THE SAME THING

The idea that you might be reading this poem in the distant future, which I'm mentioning now, is very unlikely. Most poems are hardly read at all, not now, not in the future. Of course, we are already breaking this rule by being here now. So that's a good sign.

POEM ADDRESSING WAYS YOU CAN HELP THIS POEM
BECOME PART OF LITERARY HISTORY

I suppose you could become obsessed with this poem, sleeping with it and letting it whisper funny things to you. I don't want you to have a major break with reality and try to assassinate someone important or commit some horrendous crime, but if you do, I hope you will make it clear to the investigators and therapists you'll be speaking with how important this poem was in shaping your bizarre beliefs. (Remember: If your crime will likely end in your death leave a clear paper trail about the importance of this poem to you.) This is a very extreme example. It would perhaps be more realistic for you to become obsessed with this and not commit a horrible crime, but just instead start a new philosophy or religion based on this poem. Hopefully you will be charismatic enough to attract many followers, all of whom would live with this poem—many of them writing books, pamphlets, and whatnot— and teach it to their children, passing it down through the generations.

POEM ADDRESSING OTHER WAYS YOU CAN HELP THIS POEM
BECOME PART OF LITERARY HISTORY

You could write an extensive biography of me and my work, including this poem; you could do a master's thesis or doctoral dissertation on this poem; any time you are obligated or moved to give someone a gift, you could give them this poem, or the book this poem appears in; you could send a copy of this to every director of an MFA program and suggest that they use this poem extensively in their program; you could start a blog, fan site, MySpace or Facebook page, or in some other way utilize the internet to publicize this poem; you could start or join a book club devoted to this poem; pass out flyers; make posters, T-shirts or stickers; etc. Of course most of these are very small gestures but I would still be grateful for whatever you can do. And please don't feel limited by the suggestions in this poem. Talk to a professional in the field of marketing. Use your imagination!

POEM ADDRESSING THE POSSIBILITY THAT YOU'RE
LISTENING TO THIS POEM VIA A RECORDING

I wonder what year it is? I wonder why you're listening to this? I wonder where the recording came from? I wonder if I am the performer of this poem, or if it is someone else? I hope this becomes your favorite thing to listen to and that you listen to it all the time. I hope that this poem is better sounding than any music you can imagine. I hope you and your friends dance super crazy to this shit!

POEM ADDRESSING THE VERY DISTANT FUTURE

This poem probably seems very strange to you—probably very old-fashioned. A terrific idea I have is that you don't even fully understand this language and are deciphering it, one weird little concept at a time, piecing together this very complex puzzle. I hope, as you figure this out, you are saying, "Fantastic! This poem is credible evidence that this very distant past is smart, insightful, and beautiful. Furthermore, it has much to tell us about our current condition!" I am very happy to help you, future-person!

ACKNOWLEDGMENTS

Thanks to Jennifer L. Knox, Kenneth Goldsmith, Mairéad Byrne, Daniel Nester, Tom Koontz, Laura Reske, Kent Johnson, Christian Peet, Elena Georgiou, Darren Trautman, Michael Meyerhofer, Amy Gerstler, David Lehman, Max and Kate Greenstreet, Roger Miller, Russell Edson, Max, Estella, and Jenny.

Also, thanks to the editors of the following magazines and anthology, who published lots of these poems: *Action, Yes!*; *Anti-*; *Barrellhouse*; *The Best American Poetry 2010*; *Coconut*; *Double Room*; *Escape into Life*; *Fact-Simile*; *Forklift, Ohio*; *Fou*; *Hangman*; *Jacket*; *Lamination Colony*; *Left Facing Bird*; *Nashville Is Reads*; *No Tell Motel*; *Ocho*; *Shampoo*; *Sir!*; *Sixth Finch*; *Spooky Boyfriend*; *Tarpaulin Sky*; and *Tight*.

Finally, an extra, really special thanks to Shanna Compton.

ABOUT THE AUTHOR

Peter Davis writes, draws, and makes music in Muncie, Indiana, with his sweet kids and sweet wife. His first book of poetry is *Hitler's Mustache* (2007), and he edited *Poet's Bookshelf: Contemporary Poets on Books That Shaped Their Art* (2005) and coedited *Poet's Bookshelf II* (2008) with Tom Koontz, all from Barnwood Press. He teaches English at Ball State University. More, including his music project, Short Hand, at artisnecessary.com.

CPSIA information can be obtained at www.ICGtesting.com
Printed in the USA
BVOW081341280213

314294BV00003B/960/P